CW00554112

Manipulation Mastery

A Survival Guide On How To Analyze People And Influence Them To Do Anything You Want Using Subliminal Persuasion, Dark Nlp, And Dark Cognitive Behavioral Therapy

Adam Smith

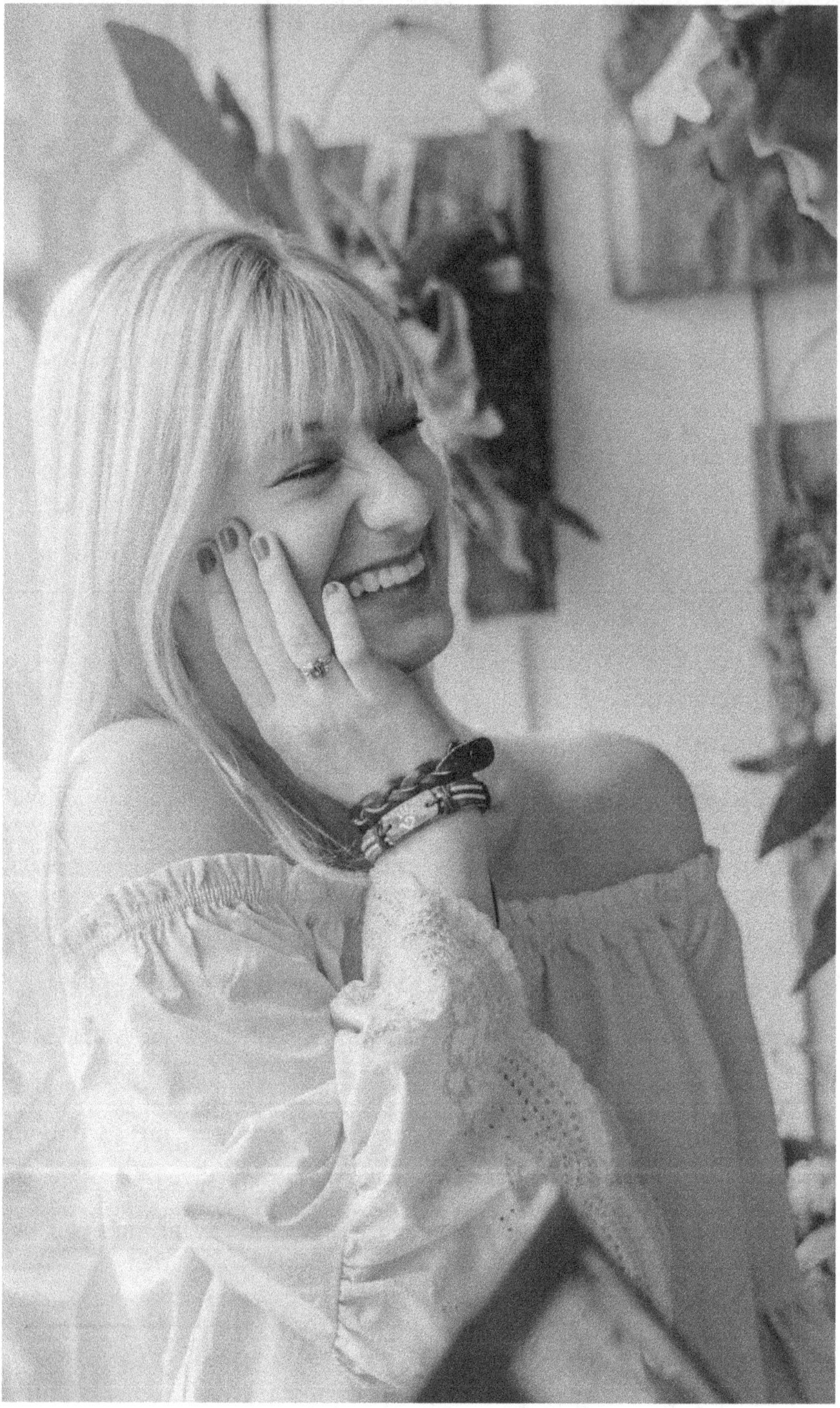

Table of Contents

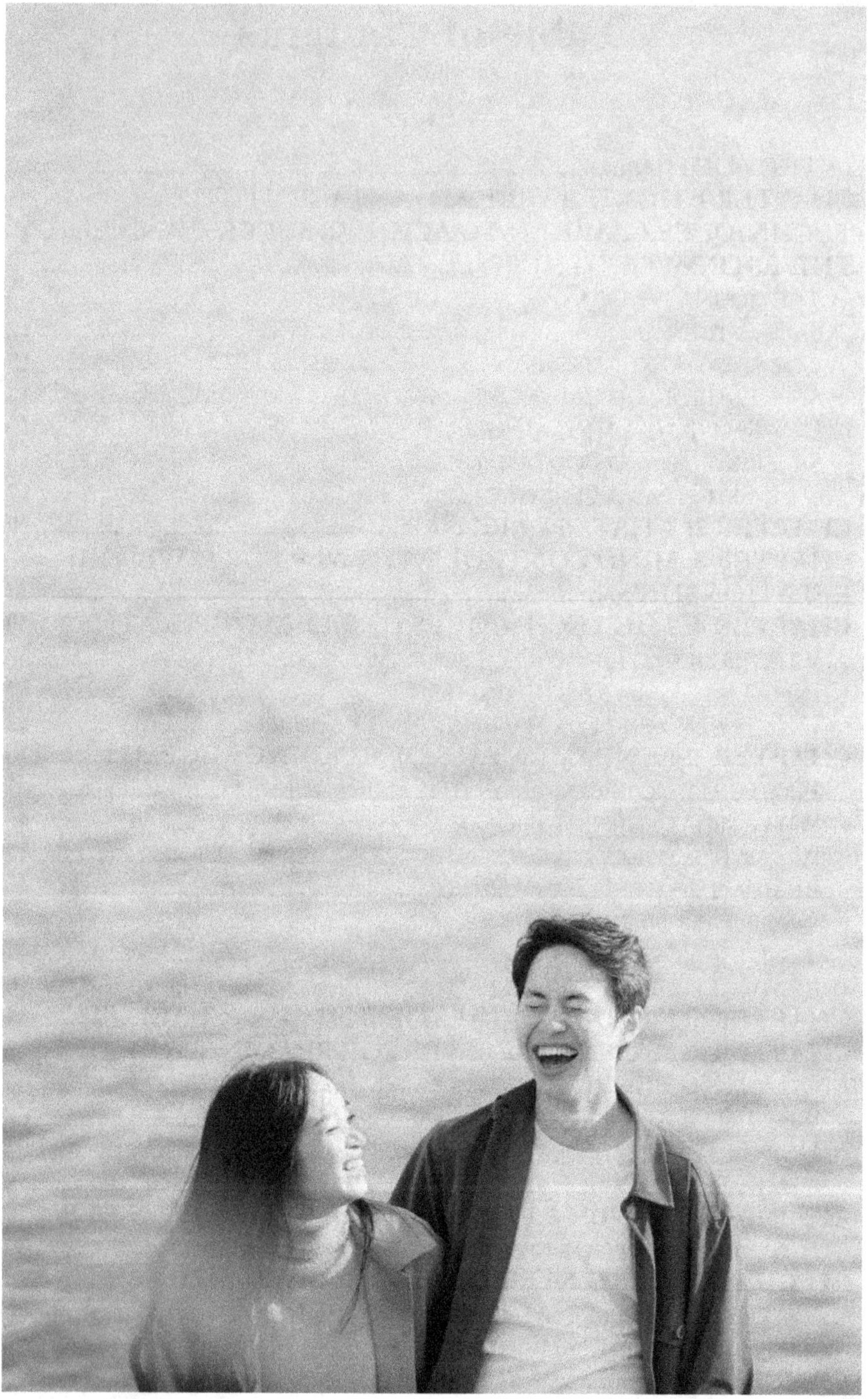

Introduction

Neuro-Linguistic Programming or NLP is known as one of the most efficient methods used by modern health specialists to help people improve their lifestyle and life in general. NLP is not really complicated to understand and use on different behavioral aspects of life which include managing anxiety, fears, and stress.

NLP is known to be a multi-dimensional process which involves behavioral capability development on top of flexibility. It also consists of tactical thinking and knowing the psychological and intellectual basis of our actions.

Experts believe NLP can be about discovering your life purpose and knowing who you really are. NLP also offers a context for understanding and connecting to the spiritual portion of the human experience. Keep in mind, changing your life for the better with NLP isn't only about skill and superiority, it's about wisdom and vision.

Here are some of the content covered in this guide;

- What is dark NLP
- Mind control with NLP for Love and relationships
- The techniques of NLP manipulation
- Fundamentals of reading people

- Fundamentals of body language

- Main guidelines for reading and analyzing people

- Manipulating the mind through NLP

- Using NLP to avoid manipulation

- Easy techniques to use NLP

- NLP Applications

- Subliminal persuasion

- Is It Possible to Take Control of Others?

- How social media plays a role in subliminal persuasion today....AND MORE!!!

Chapter 1:

How To Take Advantage Of The Techniques Learned To Achieve Success And Enjoy The Esteem Of Others

D efining the self - esteem construct is not natural, as it is a concept that has an extensive history of theoretical elaborations. A concise and shared definition in literature could be the following:

All the evaluative judgments that the individual gives of himself (Battistelli, 1994).

Three fundamental elements constantly recur in all the definitions of self - esteem (Bascelli, 2008):

- The presence in the individual of a system allows self-observation and, therefore, self-knowledge.
- An evaluative aspect allows a general judgment of oneself.
- The affective element that will enable you to evaluate and consider descriptive factors positively or negatively.

The Cognitive Construction of Self-Esteem

Self - esteem is a paradigm that can be built day by day through cognitive strategies.

A first definition of the concept of self - esteem is due to William James (cited in Bascelli and all, 2008). He conceives it as a result resulting from the comparison between the successes that the individual obtains and the expectations regarding them.

A few years later, Cooley and Mead define self-esteem as a product that arises from interactions with others, which created during life as a reflex evaluation of what other people think of us.

A person 's self - esteem does not derive exclusively from individual internal factors, but also the so-called confrontations that the individual makes, knowingly or not, with the environment in which he lives, have a positive influence.

There are two components to constitute the process of formation of self-esteem: the real self and the ideal self.

The real self is nothing but an objective view of one's abilities; it corresponds to what we are.

The ideal self-corresponds to how the individual would like to be. Self - esteem comes from the results of our experiences compared to typical expectations. The higher the discrepancy between what we are and what we would like to be, the lower our self-esteem will be.

The presence of an ideal self can be a stimulus to growth, as it induces to formulate objectives to achieve. Still, it can generate dissatisfaction and other negative emotions if you feel it very far from the real one.

To reduce this discrepancy, the individual can reduce his aspirations, and thus bring the ideal self closer to the perceived one, or he could try to improve the real person (Berti, Bombi, 2005).

Having high self-esteem is the result of a limited difference between the real self and the ideal self. It means knowing how to recognize that you have both strengths Sand weaknesses, strive to improve your weaknesses, appreciating your strengths. All this emphasizes greater openness to the environment, greater autonomy, and greater confidence in one's abilities.

People with high self-esteem show greater perseverance in succeeding in an activity they are passionate about or in achieving a goal they care about and are instead less determined in an area in which they have invested little. These are people more likely to relativize a failure and to engage in new businesses that help them forget.

On the contrary, low self-esteem can lead to reduced participation and little enthusiasm. It materializes in situations of demotivation in which disengagement and disinterest predominate. Only your weaknesses are recognized while your strengths neglected.

Often, we tend to escape even from the most trivial situations for fear of rejection by others. We are more vulnerable and less autonomous.

People with low self-esteem give up much more quickly when it comes to reaching a goal, especially if they encounter some difficulty or feel an opinion contrary to what they think.

These are people who struggle to abandon the feelings of disappointment and bitterness associated with experiencing a failure. Furthermore, in the face of criticism, they are susceptible to the intensity and duration of the discomfort caused.

But what helps to make an individual evaluate positively or negatively? Well, there is self-evaluation regarding three fundamental processes:

1. Assignment of judgments by others, both directly and indirectly. It is the so-called ' social mirror ': through the opinions communicated by significant others, we define ourselves.

2. Social confrontation: that is, the person evaluates himself by comparing himself with those around him, and from this confrontation, an evaluation arises.

3. Self-observation process: the person can also evaluate himself by observing himself and recognizing the differences between himself and others. Kelly (1955), the father of Personal Construct Psychology, for example, considers each person a 'scientist' who observes, interprets (i.e., attributes meaning to his experiences) and predicts any behavior or event, building, among other things, a self-theory to facilitate the maintenance of self-esteem.

Self-Esteem and Ideals

In practice, the central assumption of the theory is that people move through ideals and goals and monitor their path towards them, continually comparing the perception of their behavior concerning the reference standards. When the individual perceives a discrepancy between his current state and the goal, he looks for behavioral strategies to reduce this discrepancy.

People move through multiple ideal planes, and some are related to concrete habits ("ideal to go to the gym twice a week"); others are related to more abstract.

In general, the perception of a distance between how we are and how we would like to generate negative emotions of sadness, such that we led in some way to minimize this perceived difference.

However, there are two types of ideals studied: ideals adequately understood. And it is experiences, concepts, and reference standards to aim for and refer to, and contrary models (feared oneself) or situations, people (real or symbolic), goals and circumstances from which people try to distance themselves and keep away because they judge negatively.

In general, common sense and literature hypothesize a negative role of ideals on self-esteem, especially if they are too ambitious and unattainable (Marsh, 1993).

In general, it can say that despite the clear value that self-regulation towards goals has for society since it pushes the individual to improve and strive towards new goals, the run-up to ideals has individual costs in terms of mental resources and sense of one's worth.

Cognitive Distortions

Sometimes the self - analyzes that helps defines a person 's self - esteem is distorted by his cognitive distortions, that is, by thoughts that invalidate self - consideration.

Sacco and Beck (1985) indicate a series of cognitive distortions, which are:

- The cognitive inferences, through which individuals mature arbitrary ideas about themselves without the endorsement of real and objective data;
- The selective abstractions, employing which a small negative detail extrapolated, becoming symbolic and representative of one's way of being;
- The overgeneralizations, for which we led to generalize starting, for example, from a single personality trait that distinguishes an individual or from a single experiential episode that has seen him, protagonist;
- Maximization, which allows implementing the adverse effects of a single action carried out;
- Minimization, which allows reducing the definite scope of some event;

- Personalization, which authorizes one to feel guilty for some adverse event;

- The dichotomous thought does not allow nuances in the context of assumptions of responsibility, leading the analysis to the constructs of everything and nothing (black and white vision).

Self-Esteem and Causal Attributions

The process by which the individual evaluates himself is also due to causal attributions. Put more simply, and people often try to explain an event by linking it to a cause.

Usually, there is a tendency to attribute success achieved to an object external to the person, such as luck, or an internal purpose, such as tenacity.

Weiner, in 1994, said that attributions could divide into three dimensions:

- Locus of control: that is if the cause of success (or failure) is internal or external to the person

- Stability: for which the causes can be stable or unstable over time (for example, the ease of the task is steady, on the contrary luck is unstable)

- Controllability: the subject can control not all causes

It seems that the attribution to stable, controllable, and internal causes of the individual has, in the event of success, an increase in self-esteem in the individual.

On the other hand, the attribution to causes external to oneself, unstable and not very controllable, leads to a decrease in self-esteem and self - confidence.

Low Self-Esteem: Strategies to Increase It

According to Toro (2010), several strategies exist to increase the positive perception of oneself, such as:

- the increase in problem-solving skills, as self-esteem is often a function of one's ability to solve problems.

- The implementation of positive (self - talk) internal dialogue; self - esteem can be increased through positive dialogue with oneself, using one's inner voice. In other words, if we first send positive messages to our minds, self-perception is very likely to improve.

- The restructuring of the attributional style, aimed at making us achieve greater objectivity, thanks to which we could, for example, interpret the events or situations that do not depend on us as merely unfavorable.

- the improvement of self-control;

- modification of cognitive standards; by placing excessively high expectations, we run the risk of not living up to expectations and, therefore, of influencing self-perception.
- The enhancement of communication skills.

Self-Esteem and Body Image

According to the psychotherapist Luca Saita, three mechanisms would negatively interfere with the creation of the body image, namely:

- direct or indirect attack
- projection
- labeling

In the first case, the person suffers an attack, direct or not, on his own body (' You look horrible today!'). In the second case, someone, unconsciously, to get rid of their physical characteristics deemed unacceptable, attributes them to someone else (e.g., the mother who says to her daughter ' Don't put on that dress, get fat '). In the latter case, labels attributed to the person (the ' anyone, 'the ' roscio, " crooked legs ').

When a person continuously subjected to negative influences of this kind, it is no wonder that he learns to see himself only and only through the distorted lenses of disdain. The effects of such an attitude should not underestimate. The body image, the way we see and present ourselves to others, has very profound repercussions in terms of self-confidence. In other words, seeing oneself ugly, perceiving oneself inadequate has consequences. It affects not only the body but also the mind. It also affects the way of being in the world.

It is an entirely personal and subjective experience. There are, as it is possible to observe in the daily experience of each of us, people considered beautiful who, however, live as consistently inadequate and are always looking for something that is missing to feel at ease in their bodies finally. At the same time, there are people who, despite having small defects, love each other, live their bodies with serenity. And also transmit this serenity to the outside, in terms of self-confidence.

Self-Esteem and Bullying

It seems that the estimate given by ourselves can influence the phenomena of bullying. However, in literature, the relationship between self-esteem and bullying provides partly contradictory data.

Most studies seem to agree that bullied children suffer from low self-esteem, have a negative opinion of themselves and their skills (Menesini, 2000).

On the other hand, bullies often appear to be characterized by high self-esteem. In relevant research on the topic (Salmivalli, 1999) self - esteem at 14 and 15 years was investigated, and the results showed that bullies have a higher than average self - esteem, combined with narcissism and delusions of greatness. A further study showed that bullies are popular subjects, which led researchers to speculate that popularity could lead to a rise in self-esteem and aggressive conduct, as the bully would not be afraid of being sanctioned by the peer group. (Caravita, Di Balsio, 2009).

However, these data have repeatedly denied, as the fact that bullies perceive themselves as well viewed does not mean that they are. It often happens that people who have bullied behavior show themselves to be superior and powerful, but in reality, they do not think this about themselves.

The data that support the hypothesis that bullies have a positive perception of themselves believe that it is often inconsistent. For example, Salmivalli (1998) found in bullies high self-esteem concerning interpersonal relationships and physical attraction, and low self-esteem concerning school, family, behavior, and emotions (Salmivalli, 2001).

Chapter 2:

What is dark NLP

To understand Dark NLP on a theoretical level, it is first necessary to understand the ideas of NLP upon which it is based. NLP began when two individuals, Bandler and Grinder, developed a set of ideas into human behavior and how it could be influenced that came to be known as neuro-linguistic programming, more commonly known as NLP.

At first, the techniques were fairly unknown, but received wider exposure through the years through the work of superstars such as Tony Robbins and Derren Brown. Although more people than ever before have heard of NLP, very few know how to actually apply it.

The basic concepts of NLP came from the modeling of human behavior combined with linguistic principles taken from academics such as Noam Chomsky.

These two central influences are combined into a set of formal principles into the motivations of humans and how these can be influenced and modeled. One of the founders of NLP has summarized its area of focus as formalizing the concepts and principles which drive human behavior.

NLP has three main areas through which its ideas are filtered -

subjectivity, consciousness and learning. NLP teaches that there is no absolute, objective understanding of the world around us, yet instead every individual forms their own personal picture of the world which consists of the data taken in through the five senses as well as the language the person learns to attach to their sensory data.

It is theorized that this combination of sensory input and descriptive language eventually leads to behaviors that are either effective according to our subjective map of the world, or maladaptive and harmful to our own aims and pursuits.

One area in which NLP is relatively in agreement with mainstream psychology is its understanding of the human mind as having both a conscious and an unconscious dimension. Much of the teaching of NLP is predicated upon the belief that a lot of influence occurs at the subconscious level of human thought. People are vulnerable to being manipulated in ways they are not able to perceive.

NLP sees people as behaving according to three key aspects - the 'what', the 'how' and the 'why'. The 'what' focuses on the external behavior and physiology a person exhibits in a given situation, the 'how' deals with the internal thinking patterns the person has that govern their pattern of decision making, and the 'why' deals with the supporting beliefs, assumptions and values that point a person in one direction rather than another.

If you are able to understand the aforementioned three aspects then you are able to effectively model the complete reality of someone else's behavior. It should be stressed that it is the internal process that is being copied which leads to the external behavior, rather than just crudely mimicking the external behavior alone. Without the accompanying internal dimensions, the behavior is likely to come off as insincere and phony.

NLP advocates going beyond passively accepting the various factors that compromise a person's behavior. Instead, it advocates actively exploring and manipulating the variables at hand in order to understand the relationship between each, and which are essential to achieve the desired result.

There is a clear contrast between the NLP model of understanding behaviors and the traditional view. Traditionally, people acquire a new behavior by acquiring one piece of a skill at a time, until they add up to form the entire behavior. NLP instead focuses on doing things the opposite way, meaning the person is initially presented with all of the components of a behavior at once, and then proceeds to subtract various parts until they are left with only the essential aspects.

This process of simplifying behaviors and reducing them to only their crucial aspects is similar to business processes which aim to map out a series of steps and identify which are essential and which are not. In this sense, the process of refining behaviors through the application of NLP can be seen as a means of ensuring personal efficiency.

NLP also concerns itself with the question of finding the difference between two types of people within any given field - those that succeed and those who do not. Success modeling seeks to find exactly what previously successful people did in contrast from someone who failed in the same area of life. Did they think about the problem differently? Did they perceive decisions differently? Was there some behavioral habit that helped to make the difference to their results?

Chapter 3:

Mind control with NLP for Love and relationships

M ind control is used in relationships and you can do too, to get what you want from it but then you will need to be genuine when you are making use of it and you shouldn't do so just to harm your partner. For instance, you want to be able to establish a particular routine with your wife or your girlfriend where you can have your friends over to the house for a football game or for a night of gaming, on a regular basis. You just want to chill with your guys, but somehow your relationship has taken away this kind of fun from you.

If you start complaining about this to your partner, then it will just cause a lot of unnecessary friction. Instead when you make use of mind control in such a situation it is highly likely that you will get what you want without hurting anyone or your relationship. You can start by thinking of all the different activities that your partner used to do with her friends but don't disclose your plans at this stage. This is the stage for you to observe. Perhaps while watching TV, you can behave like you were prompted by the TV ads and say something like "Didn't you used to go for yoga classes?" or something similar like that. Even she would have given up on a few things for the sake of the relationship and you will need to take note of those things. She would naturally want to feel loved and appreciated. If you give her the impression that you are also willing to make a few sacrifices so that she can get back to doing what she used to enjoy and this will incidentally coincide with the activity that you want to do, but in this case you are taking the initiative.

As soon as she agrees to something ad says that she would be very happy that she could do what she wants, you needn't jump in with your predefined plans at this stage. You will need to wait for a while. She will start feeling guilty that you are at home working while she is out having fun doing what she likes. You will need to keep building up the drama as well as the scene so that the inevitable comes, unless she is extremely selfish, her natural response would be that it doesn't seem fair that she is going out to have fun and that you are confined to the house.

Now, this is the perfect time for you to put up the idea that you could perhaps have your friends over and now she can't eve complain or restrict you from doing it because she was the one who had suggested that in the first place and in her mind you are definitely doing something that would be equivalent of what she does to be happy. The thing with mind control is that you will need to look at all the different angles and the different scenarios in which you can make use of NLP and Environmental control models. By making use of this approach you will be able to see the bigger picture and you can stay in control of it. You will be able to manipulate the situation in such a manner that by the end of the day you get to do what you have wanted to do but also you have made your partner extremely happy for you that she did and she might also take credit for doing so. It can work in multiple ways for a relationship.

Sometimes you can make sue of reverse psychology as well. Parents tend to make use of isolation as a form of punishing a child. If the child does something wrong they would put the child in isolation where they are in fact giving the child an exclusive behavior. If the child wants to keep that bedroom all to her and not have to share it with others, she can regularly act in the manner that will get her to the bedroom. In this situation, the power actually lies with the child and not the parents, but they don't know that, do they? Everyone has got this ability within themselves; all they need to do is to act on it. In relationships, you will need to think about the things that you want to achieve, the reaction of others to this and the ones you are in a close relationship with. Then you can start thinking of the ways in which you can make this viable and also think about what they want. It works like magic in one on one relationships because you will definitely know what your partner would be likely thinking in a particular situation, then all that you will need to do is mold the situation in such a manner that it will turn their thought process towards the set direction in which you want them to think, without their knowledge that this is exactly what you want them to do. This is exactly what advertisers keep doing. They continually keep changing people's allegiances from one product to another and from one brand to another.

Everyone wants to have whiter teeth, so the thing that you, as a marketer would need to do is make a product and then make people think that this particular product will help them get whiter teeth, thereby fulfilling their need to be accepted into the society. Similarly, other advertisements for products work on the notion that you are conscious about your looks and that the product they are marketing will make you feel better about yourself. You will need to start controlling the mindset of the society, because once you are able to do this, then you will be able to control the mind successfully. If you want to get a huge LCD TV, but you know that your wife is against it, and then you will need to come up with a clever plan, one in which your wife will get to realize the benefits of having such a big TV and voila. You will get what you wished for.

The one thing that you will need to understand is that mind control should be used for the greater good. For instance, if you really want to have boy's nights then come up with a situation where even your girl gets to do what she likes and this will make her happy as well as you. This would be a win-win for both the parties involved. If you knew that your partner was feeling very low or extremely optional, do not approach this situation with mind control. Sit her down and have a long conversation about what made her emotional. Don't try to manipulate such a situation. Come up with solutions and plant the seeds so that your partner can also come up with the same solutions on their own accord. Why do you need to do this? By doing this you will be able to ensure that even a person who isn't open to new ideas might come to accept them. You will need to plant the seeds and just leave them at that. Let the person whose mind you are trying to control discover those seeds. In this manner you will be able to reap the benefits when all you have down is just sowed the seeds. In this manner you would have achieved what you want without being intrusive. The seeds of an idea can be very subtly planted. You don't need to shout them out at the top of your voice. For instance, you want a new laptop, but your partner thinks that it's a sheer waste of money. Play some music on it or suggest that the two of you can watch a movie on it.

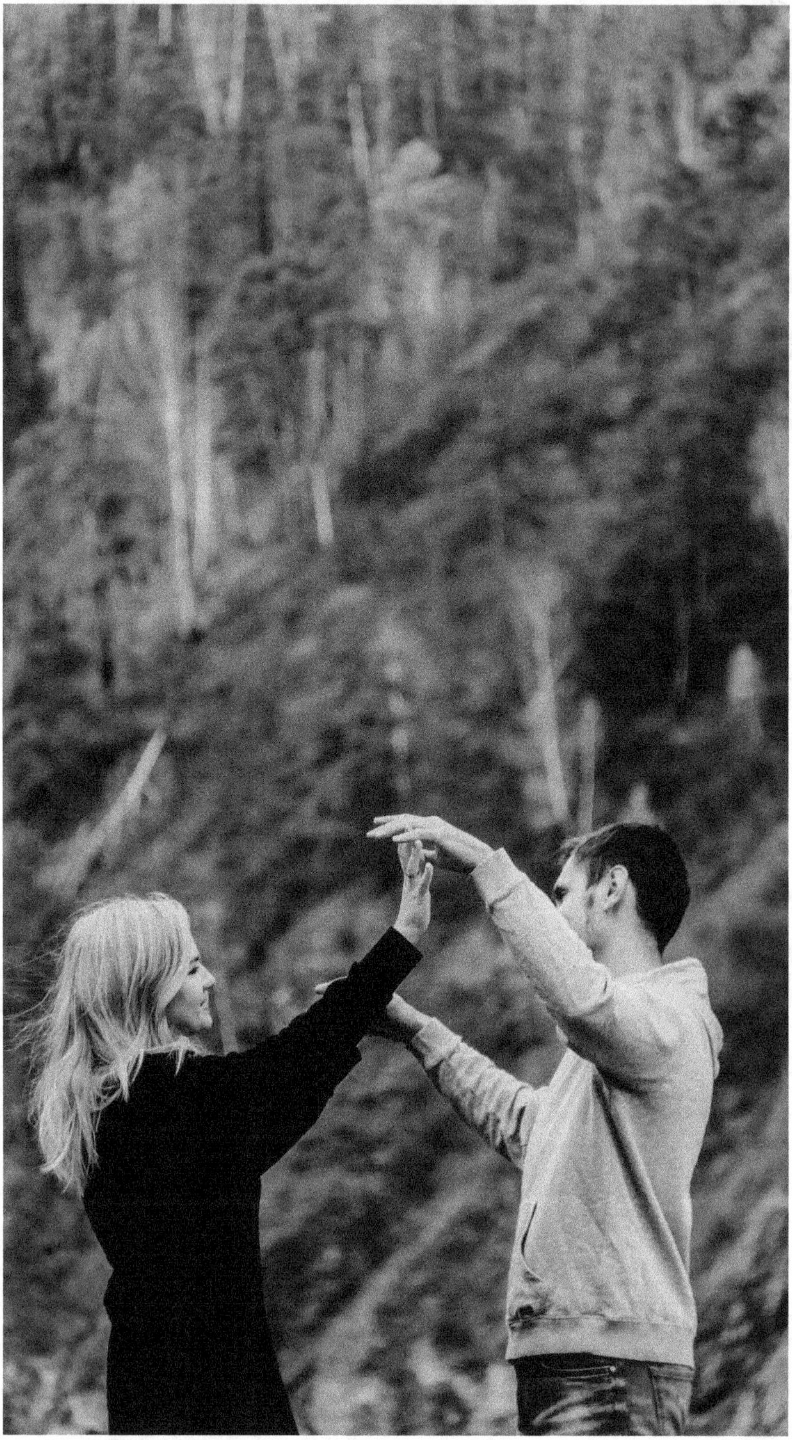

Chapter 4:

The techniques of NLP manipulation

What is Neuro Linguistic Programming?

Neuro Linguistic Programming, or NLP, in simplest terms is the programming language of your mind. We've all had instances where we attempted to communicate with someone who doesn't speak our language. The outcome? They didn't understand us!

You go to a restaurant abroad and ask for a fancy steak but end up receiving insipid stew owing to the misinterpretation of language and codes.

This is precisely what happens when we try to communicate with our subconscious mind. We think we are commanding it to give us happier relationships, more money, a better job and other, similar things. However, if that's not what is actually showing up, something is being lost in translation. The subconscious/unconscious mind has the power to help us accomplish our goals only if we program it using codes it recognizes and understands.

If you are asking your unconscious mind for steak and receiving stew, it is time to speak its language. Think of NLP as a user manual for the brain. When people master NLP, they become fluent in the language of the subconscious mind, which is excellent when it comes to re-programming their own and other people's thoughts, ideas and beliefs. This gives them the power to influence and persuade people, and on the downside, even manipulate them.

Neuro Linguistic Programming is a set of techniques, methods and tools for enhancing communication with deeper layers of our brain. It is an approach that combines personal development, psychotherapy and communication. Its creators (John Grinder and Richard Bandler) claim that there is a strong link between language, behavior patterns and neurological processes, which can be used for enhancing learning and personal development.

Influence versus Manipulation

So, do you believe a hammer is a tool of utility or destruction? Well, it depends on how you use it, right? Or what purpose you use it for.

NLP is potent when it comes to getting people to do what you want them to. It is the hammer that can be used to fix a nail in the wall or destroy a piece of wood. Similarly, NLP can be used to build something positive, or it can be used for a destructive purpose (manipulation).

NLP and manipulation have nearly the same meaning. Both are about generating the desired effect on other people without obvious exertion. However, one key difference between influence and manipulation is that the latter is meant to influence others to meet the manipulator's selfish goals through means that can be unfair, unlawful, sneaky, or insidious. Things are contrived through underhanded methods to turn out in favor of the manipulator. A manipulator often preys on the insecurities, fears and guilt of other people. In turn, victims of manipulation feed dissatisfied, frustrated, trapped and unhappy.

Conversely, influence is the ability to inspire people in an admirable, charismatic and honorable way. We are often inspired by influential people and aspire to model our life on theirs. There is a general feeling of positivity related to them, and we feel positively impacted in their company. Not every influence is positive, which is why we use terms such as "bad influence" to signify a person's negative effect on us. However, manipulation is never categorized as good or bad. It always operates with sinister motives. That is the primary difference between influence and manipulation.

Influence is a double-edged sword that can be used positively and negatively, while manipulation only operates with a negative, narrow and selfish perspective to meet the objectives of the manipulator.

While manipulation has self-centered and questionable motives, influence can also be positive. In contrast to manipulation, influence has positive connotations, which considers other people's needs, goals and desires. Don't we, as parents, want to influence our children to lead happier and healthier lives? Similarly, as a manager, we want to influence our team to put in their best efforts.

Just like the hammer discussed above, people can use NLP for positively or negatively influencing people to meet their own selfish objectives (manipulation). NLP is a mind control tool that can do both – build and damage.

How is NLP Used for Manipulating People?

NLP training is conducted in a pyramid-like structure, with sophisticated techniques reserved for high-end seminars. It is a complex subject (whoever said anything related to the human mind would be easy?). However, to simplify a complicated concept, NLPers, or people who practice NLP, pay keen attention to people they work with. They watch everything from eye movements to skin flushes to pupil dilation in order to determine what type of information people are processing.

Through observation, NLPers can tell which side of the brain is dominant in a person. Similarly, they can tell what sense is the most active within the person's brain. The eye movements can determine how their brain stores and uses information. It is also easy to decipher whether the person is stating facts (telling the truth) or making up facts (lying) by looking at his/her eye movements.

After gathering this invaluable information, NLP manipulators will subtly mirror and mimic their victims (including speech, body language, mannerisms, verbal linguistic patterns and more) to give a feeling of being 'one among them.'

NLPers will fake social clues to lead their victims into dropping their guard and entering a more open, receptive and suggestible state of mind, where they become ready to absorb whatever information their mind is fed. Manipulators will cleverly use language that focuses on a person's predominant senses.

For example, if a person is focused on his/her visual sense, the NLP manipulator will most likely use it to his/her advantage optimally by saying something like, "Do you see where I am coming from?" "Can you see what I am trying to tell you?" or "See it this way?" Similarly, if a person is a predominantly auditory person, the manipulator will speak to them using auditory metaphors like, "Just hear me out once, Tim" or "I hear you."

By mirroring their victim's body language and verbal linguistic patterns, NLP experts, or NLPer manipulators, attempt to accomplish a clear objective – building rapport. As discussed earlier, manipulators also try to accomplish this by sharing too much too soon or building early intimacy. The objective is the same – to strike a rapport with their victims, which then makes it easy for the victims to let down their guard.

Once the manipulator uses NLP to build rapport and get the victim to let down his guard through clever use of body language and verbal patterns, the victim becomes more open and suggestible. Fake social cues are fed to the victim to make their minds more malleable.

Once they build a rapport, NLPers will begin to lead the victim into increased interaction in a sublime manner. After having mirrored the victim and establishing in the victim's subconscious mind that he/she (the manipulator) is one among them (the victim), the manipulator increases his/her chances of getting the victim to do whatever the manipulator wants. They will subtly change their behavior and language to influence their victim's actions.

The techniques can include leading questions, sublime language patterns and a host of other NLP techniques to maneuver the person's mind wherever they want. The victim, on the other hand, often doesn't realize what is happening. In their view, everything is occurring naturally/organically or according to their consent.

Of course, manipulators (however skilled) may not be able to use NLP to get people to behave in a manner that is completely out of character. However, it can be used to steer people's responses in the desired direction. For instance, you can't convince a fundamentally ethical and truthful person to act in a dishonest manner. However, you can use it to get a person to think in a specific direction or line of thought. Manipulators use NLP to engineer specific responses from a person.

NLP attempts accomplish two ends, eliciting and anchoring. Eliciting occurs when NLPers use language and leading to draw their victims into an emotional state. Once the desired state is accomplished, the NLPer will then anchor the emotion with a specific physical clue - for example, tapping on their shoulder. This simply means that an NLPer can invoke the same emotion in you by tapping your shoulder.

For example, let us say the NLP manipulator makes you feel depressed or unworthy using language, leading and other NLP techniques. This is followed by tapping the back of your hands in a specific manner to create anchoring. Thus, each time they want to create an emotion of being disillusioned, depressed and unworthy in you, they will tap the back of your palm. It is nothing but conditioning you to feel in a certain way with linked physical clues.

Now that you have a fair idea of what NLP is or how manipulators can use it for submission, what can you do to guard yourself against NLP manipulators?

Here are some tips to prevent NLPers from pulling their remarkably smart yet sneaky tricks on you:

1. Be wary of people mirroring your body language. Agreed, you didn't know this until now, but people imitating or copying your body language is one of the biggest red flags of them trying to manipulate, influence or persuade you to act in a desired manner. I really enjoy testing these NLP experts using subtle hand gestures and leg movements to gauge if they are indeed mirroring my body language to establish a rapport.

If they follow suit, that's my clue to flee! Experienced NLPers have mastered the art of subtle mirroring, which means you may not even realize they are imitating your actions. NLP beginners will instantly imitate the exact same movement in their eagerness to establish a feeling of oneness. Good way for you to call their bluff!

2. Confuse with eye movements. Another fantastic way to call an NLP manipulator's bluff is to notice if they are paying very close attention to your eyes or eye movements. NLP users often examine their target or victim's very carefully. The eye movements are scrutinized to gauge how you access and store information.

In effect, they want to determine what parts of the brain you are utilizing to gather clues about your thoughts and feelings. I say beat this by darting your eyes all around the place randomly. Move them upwards and downwards or from side to side in no clear pattern. You are throwing your NLP manipulator off course. Make it appear natural. Their calibration will go down the wayside.

3. Beware of people's touch. One of the techniques NLPers use is anchoring. If you know a person practices NLP, and you are in an especially heightened or intense emotional condition, do not allow them to touch you in any manner. Just throw them off course by suddenly laughing hard or flying into a fit of rage. Basically, you are confusing them about the emotion they need to anchor. Even if they attempt to establish a physical clue to invoke certain emotions, they'll be left with a mixed bag of crazy laughter, rage and whatever else you did.

4. Watch out for permissive language. Typical language used by NLPers includes "be relaxed," "relax and enjoy this," and other similar statements. Beware of this NLP, hypnotist style language that induces

you into a state of deep relaxation or trance to get you to think or act in a specific manner. Skilled or covert manipulators rarely command in a straightforward manner.

They will cleverly seek your permission to give you the impression that you are doing what they want you to do out of your own free will (one of their many sinister tricks). If you observe experienced hypnotists, they will never outright command you to do anything but seek your permission to make it appear as if it is being done organically, with your consent.

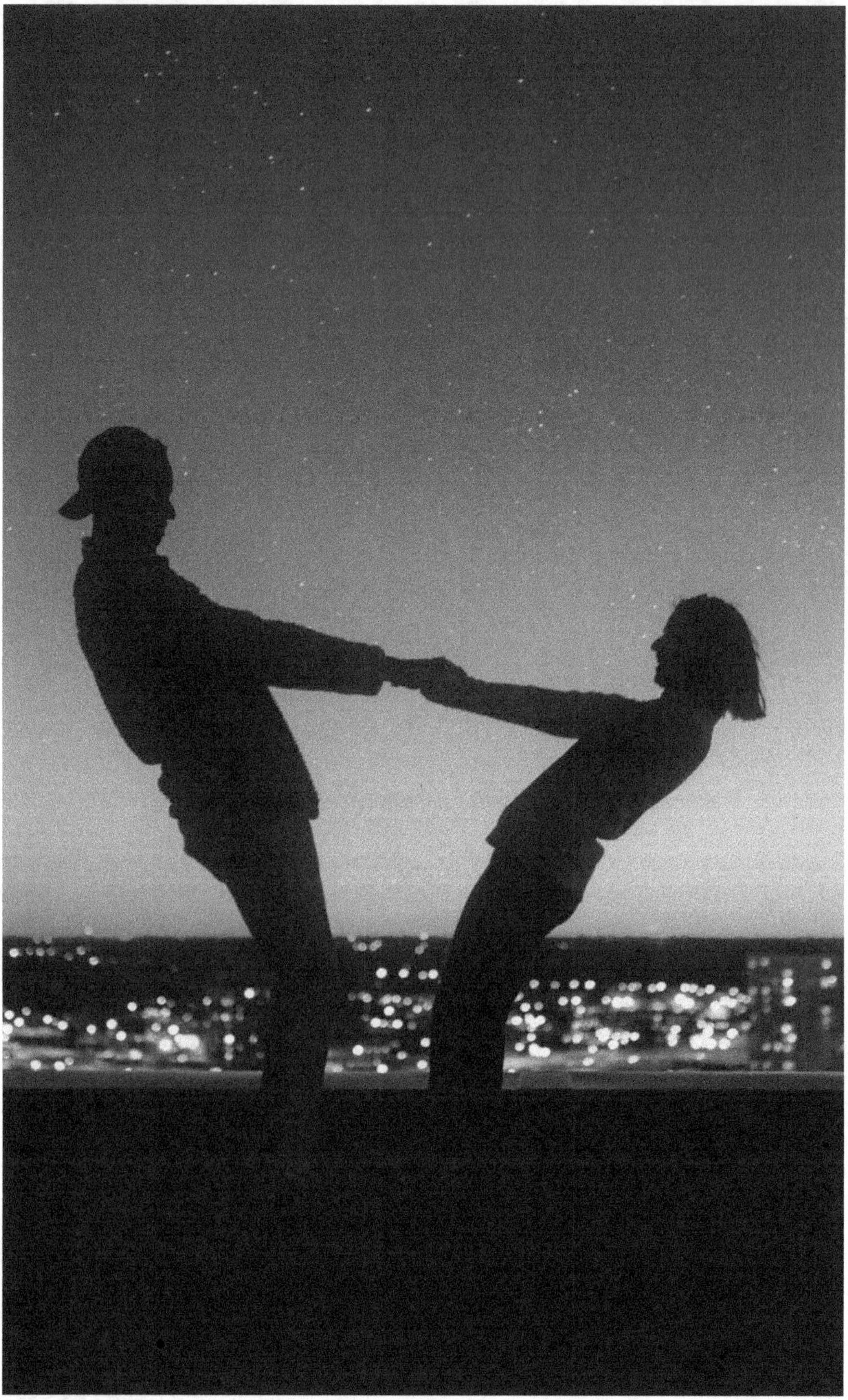

Chapter 5:

Fundamentals of reading people

Being able to analyze people can be a hard nut to crack, as it requires a lot of mental work. From studying the body languages to understanding facial expressions, and how to manage the emotions expressed by people and their egos. It takes a huge amount to analyze people. However, the mental work and activities required can only be possible if you are able to read people, and not just read, you have to be excellent at it too.

The ability and capacity to be able to read people is something that you have to develop with constant practice, and it is just like every other thing in the world, some people are much better at it than other people. Quite naturally, the people who have acquired knowledge, combined with real-world practice are essentially the best people at it. Reading people is a natural act and humans being social creatures are wired to read and study people every time we interact with each other.

People are involved in the proceedings of this world and in studying them, they could either cooperate or not want to. However, even when people think they are not giving you the chance to study them in order to be able to analyze them better, they still are. Sitting alone in the corner of the room away from everyone also requires cooperation on some level with the society.

For instance, some nations are not attempting to war each other, because of the interconnected network of human behavior designed to instill peace and harmony functions as it should. Therefore, it is essentially the cooperation and behavior of several people cooperating together on some level by essentially, keeping away from participating in acts that might lead to harm in another person,

People are not as good as they think they are

When you come in contact with a stranger, how long does it take you to evaluate the individual before you arrive at your first impression?

Several people believe it took them less than a minute to do this, however, science has found that it takes a lot less time than people believe it to be. Psychologists at Princeton University have established through several studies on the subject that it takes an individual only about one-tenth of a second to make the first judgment of someone, and it is primarily based on the body language of the other person.

Dr. Albert Mehrabian discussed a fact in one of his books that only about 7% of communication is made through the use of words, while the remaining 93% is as a result of vocal clues and nonverbal messages such as posture, gestures and facial expressions among others.

Simply put, you need to be aware of the way people come across to you and how you come across to them, as they form the vast majority of human interaction. Being able to identify these cues could either make or break the career of a budding professional.

If you are looking to move up the ladder in a social situation, be it at work, in your community etc., you have to be able to harness the knowledge of body language and nonverbal cues, as they provide you with a huge advantage in both professional and non-professional circumstances. The ability to speed-read and analyze people accurately could be what stands between you impressing the people you look up to and embarrassing the people around you.

All of these, however, brings to mind an important question, how exactly can you improve your ability to read people?

What are you doing wrong?

Before we go on to answer the question "how to improve your ability to read people?" We first need to establish the things you are doing wrong, so that these discrepancies will cease to come up, and you will be able to read people better.

There are some common errors that people make in a bid to understand people and read them better. These errors may include:

Ignoring Context. This is an important fact people tend to overlook. The context in which the nonverbal clue is bring expressed do matter a lot. The fact that you have your arms crossed, do not necessarily indicate that the room is cold or the chair you are sitting on does not have armrests. A good number of times, things have to go beyond the common-sense situations attached to the environment. It is therefore essential to ask yourself the question: "Should someone in this situation act in this manner?" You should remember that the arms might be crossed in a bid to fend off danger or simply to hide, or protect the torso, it might be crossed in order for the individual to self-reassure his/herself, or because the individual is angry. Always make sure to include the context in which the individual is exhibiting these cues.

Not looking for clusters. This happens to be one of the biggest mistakes you can make. Looking for a single tell might be great in movies, but it is different in real life. In real life, it is more about a consistent grouping of actions. An example of such is the case of poker players, rather than the single tell described in movies, a consistent grouping of actions which include sweating, touching the face and stuttering together describes what you might find, to be meaningful. It is therefore essential to ask the question: Are most of the behaviors exhibited by this person associated with "X"? For instance, an angry person will not cross his arms alone, he would probably frown and fume and exhibit a group of behaviors that will indicate anger.

Not establishing a baseline. Baselines are essential if you are to know for certain the nonverbal and verbal behaviors exhibited by an individual. The fact that the individual is jumpy does not indicate anything. However, if the individual is always jumpy and then suddenly stops moving, you should ask yourself the question: "Is this the normal way they act?" When you do not establish a baseline with which new behaviors can be compared, it will be difficult to understand and ascertain if the behavior being exhibited is normal to the individual, or not.

Not being conscious of Biases. The first impression you make of an individual is bound to affect your judgment of the person. If you already like or dislike, the individual, then you are bound to judge based on it. If the people who come close to you and often compliment you are the same people you like and approve of, it just might sway you unconsciously. It will also be a long while before you can become impressed by people you do not approve of. (Saying these tricks do not apply to you is also a bias. The biggest bias of all occurs when you think you are unbiased).

Why is it important to know how to read people?

Being able to read people comes with its benefits and it is so much more than playing Sherlock Holmes. It is about observing the people you communicate with and adjusting the manner with which you communicate with them.

In every area of life, there are a myriad of personality types to deal with, and it is essential to be able to recognize them if we are going to tap into their strengths. For instance, if you have an employee or a friend you observe to have low self-esteem or lacks self-confidence, you should be able to adjust your tone in order to accommodate their insecurities in a way that motivates them. It would be wrong and inefficient if you were to be loud and boisterous in your manner of dealing with them. However, if the individual you are dealing with is an extrovert, then being solemn and serious is an inefficient way of getting through to them.

The world of today disconnects us from one another and even nature than ever before. Today, we hardly make eye-contact with the barista who hands us our coffee over the counter. The power of observation and the need to read people accurately is therefore not necessary for communicating effectively. It is only a tool that helps to promote the connection between us as human beings.

Reading People

The ability to read people has more to do with nonverbal communication and body language alone. The essential things to look at before you can successfully read people include posture, gestures, physical movements, the person's appearance, facial expressions, the tone of voice and willingness to make eye contact during conversations etc. There is a study that finds that you can read someone only 7% from the words they say, 38% from their vocal clue, such as tone, pitch and volume and finally, 55% from their body language. The study was however focused on reading someone on a first impression basis.

You also have to consider the context in which the behaviors are being exhibited, personality and the possibility that anybody might try to deceive you by manipulating the communication.

These clues, however, do not make you privy to the innermost thoughts and feelings of other people, however, if you are observant, then you will be able to read their body language. The following include some steps to take in order to be able to read people better.

Establish a baseline

Majority of people have different behavioral quirks and sometimes these quirks are habitual. Examples include clearing their throat, scratching their head, stroking their necks and so on. It is, however, essential that you read and understand what the normal behavior of the person is, and that is your baseline

Know the person. In order to be able to read a person better, you have to establish a baseline and to establish a baseline, you have to know the person well. By getting to know them personally, you are going to have a better idea of the things they like and dislike, their behavioral habits etc. Also, you have to pay attention to the individuals and their habits, even the littlest habits, such as eye gaze, fluttering the eyes etc. This will help you in noting the things to look for when you are analyzing them.

It is essential then to base your opinions of other people on several of your encounters with them, not just one because sometimes situations determine the actions and mannerisms of everyone. For instance, one of your friends may be very fidgety. Fidgeting would normally be a sign of nervousness or dishonesty, but in this individual, it is a natural habit. If you had not been the friend of the individual and just came across them on the street, your impression of them would be nervous or anxious which in reality is wrong.

Ask open-ended questions. During the process of reading someone, what you are doing is watching and listening. What you are not doing, however, is taking control of the conversation and steering it in your direction. Ask your question straight and make your conclusions.

Open-ended questions will give the individual room to talk more, allowing you to observe them for a longer time. When you ask questions that are not straight to the point, you may get a rambling reply that may not provide you with adequate information.

Look for inconsistencies in their baseline. It is also important to seek out the discrepancies in the baseline. For instance, when a normally affectionate person turns out to not be physically present anymore and does not seem to want to be close to anyone, then you should know that something is up with such person.

Once you identify the individual's daily pattern of behavior, be on the lookout for events or behaviors that stand out. In the example of the affectionate person, when you ask why s/he suddenly becomes aloof, you may find that it is because they: are exhausted, got in a fight with other people, or other personal issues that bothers them.

Work in Clusters. Identifying only one cue is not enough reason to make conclusions. For instance, someone could lean away from you because the chair on which they are sitting is hard to be comfortable in. Even if you are focused on their nonverbal behavior, make sure to identify between three and four different signs before you make conclusions. You can take a cue from their tone, their body, their face, and their words. If you can get one from each, then it may be safe to make assumptions.

Identify your own weaknesses. "It is the nature of man to err." This statement indicates the vulnerability of human and their fallibility. Everybody likes pretty things, even the Pope, and the odds are when you identify something as pretty, you are going to like it, even if the something "pretty" is dangerous. As humans, we generally think of the drunks that roam the street with a knife as dangerous, when in reality, most psychopaths are charming and orderly. Even though it is virtually impossible to control this thought of yours, be aware of the tendency your subconscious possess to have you judge a book by its cover when it may not be the best or most accurate thing to do.

Register Vocal Cues.

It is important that you pay attention to the vocal cues exhibited by the individual during the course of your conversation.

Listen to the tone of voice. The voice of an individual is enough to tell you about the way the individual feels. Watch out for the inconsistencies that may arise in their tone or the pitch of their voice. Do they sound angry and happy? Do they sound tired and happy? If the answer to these questions is yes, then they are probably making attempts to cover things up.

When paying attention to the voice, note the volume also, do they talk louder or quieter than is normal for them? Also, watch out for such expressions as "um" or "uh," do they use them often? If the answer is yes, again, then the individual might be nervous or lying and delaying. Make sure to note if their tone, however, transmits an emotion they are not expressing totally. For example, do these people sound angry or sarcastic? They may feel the need to address what is going on in a passive manner.

Note the tone and length of their responses. When the responses you are being offered are short and clipped, it could mean that the individual is either busy or frustrated. If the responses are, however, long, then that means that the person is interested and would like to go on with the conversation.

Consider the choice of words. When people talk about things, there is often a process behind the content. For instance, if a friend said to you, you are dating another nurse?" The fact that they used the word "another" suggests that what they really mean is "Oh, but you just dated a nurse and see where that led to, now you are dating another one."

Of recent, people have used the construction "yeah, no." These two words indicate ambivalence and are also used to indicate definiteness, assent or dissent or anything at all. If your friend says to you, Dude, Come on." The "dude" in the statement indicates solidarity by saying, friend. Begin analyzing the words of the individual in order to indicate how they feel truly.

Reading people in different contexts.

There are different contexts in which you communicate with people. All contexts, however, require you to analyze the other person in order to become more connected and understand then better. The way you would read your partner on a date would be different from the way you would read your interviewer.

Know the appropriate clues in a romantic context. When you are on a date, you might want to be sure that the other person is attracted to you and also, is interested in you., again it is essential to read the clues in clusters and not as one. It is a common occurrence for people, especially women, to be mistaken as being interested when they are only friendly, so stay alert and watch out for the clues.

Watch out for the body language they exhibit. Do they lean forward? Is their body language relaxed (i.e. are their arms not crossed or shoulders tensed)? When these signs are present, it shows that the person feels comfortable with you and is probably interested in you. Also, try to notice the frequency with which the other person talks and how immersed they are in the conversation.

If they are interested in the conversation, they would nod when you talk, lean forward and ask questions. Also, notice the rate at which they smile, if they, however, seem tense and do not smile the entire time, it may suggest that they do not feel comfortable. At the end of the day, notice how they approach you. It is at this time that you should be aware of interactions that deal with touch., as this will give you an insight into how they feel towards you.

Know the constructs of a job interview. Partaking in a job interview can be nerve-wracking and at the end of it all, it is often difficult to ascertain how well one performed. You should keep an eye out for body languages, as they may mean that the interview is going on well. However, also know that in this context, both the interviewer and interviewee are alert.

You might want to watch out for body languages such as the interviewer leaning in and asking questions. You want them to show that they are interested in you and the things you have to say. However, if your interviewer shuffle papers, check his or her phone or computer screen, this may suggest that they are losing interest. You should attempt to recapture their attention if they appear to be getting impatient or bored.

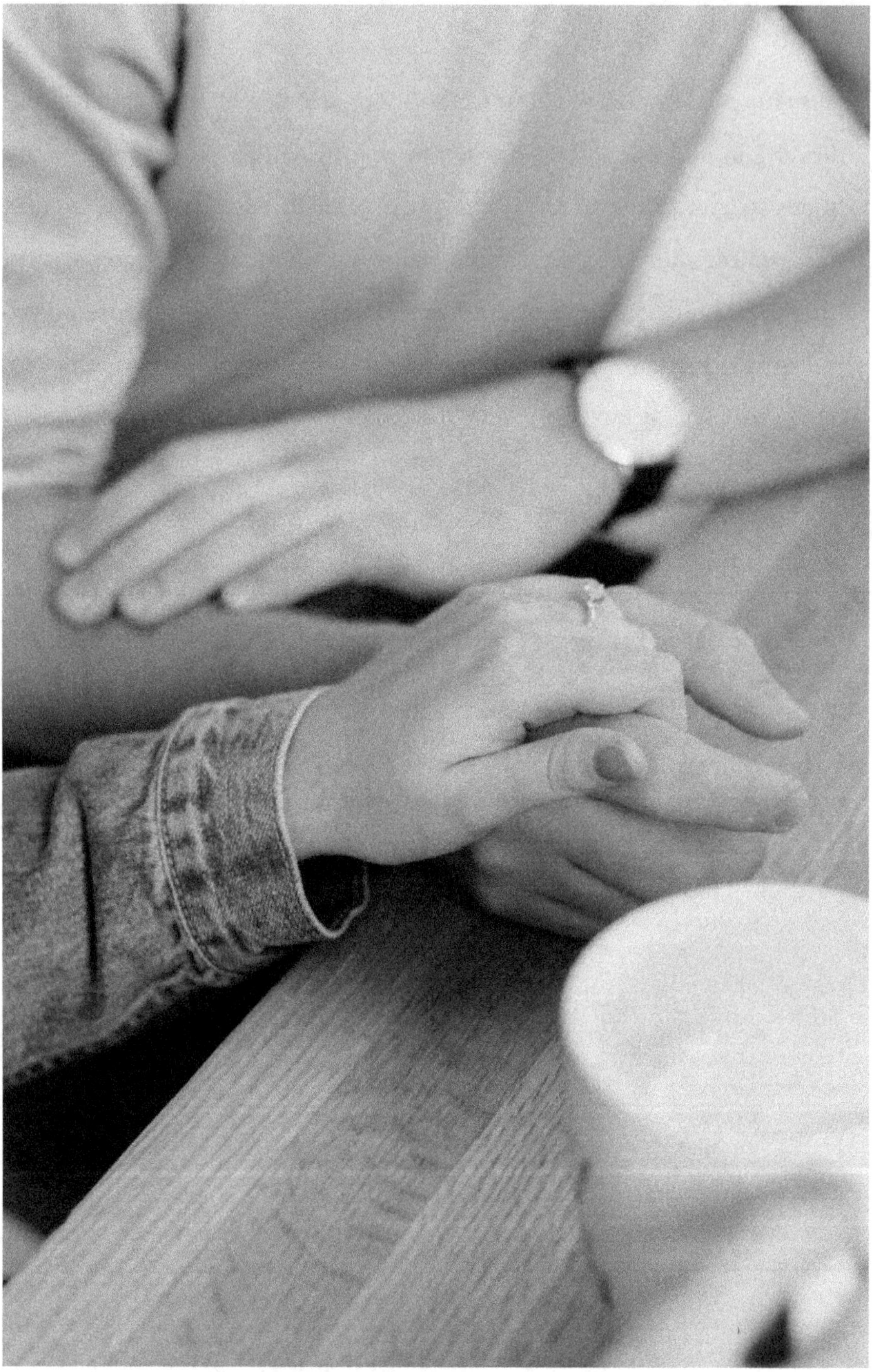

Chapter 6:

Fundamentals of body language

Body language is a main form of communication and you can get so much more from paying attention to body language than you can with any other form of communication. A person's body doesn't lie.

If they are perturbed, their body will show it. If they're angry, the body will show it. The body will show what a person does and doesn't want to do, if they are tired, interested, bored, etc.

Body language is part of our everyday transactions and interactions. You probably already observe and analyze so much more body language than you think. If you are walking and you see a certain swing in the hips in another person, this can be enough to give you a whole idea about what that person wants.

A small change in eye direction can be a huge mark of body language. These are very subtle movements that result in the transmission of ideas and attitudes.

If you have any experience with acting, you know that how a person leads with their body can tell you about their personality. If a person "leads" with one part of their body, you might notice it in how they walk; one person might lead with their head, and you will notice that will be the most prominent part of the body as they transport themselves. Another person might lead with the hips. People tend to accentuate one part of their body when walking, and this can tell you a little something about their personality.

For example, if a person is leading with their hips, you might find that they are a particularly sexual person and that sexual and sensual drives are how they make their way in the world and how they use their bodies and minds in space. If a person leads with their head, you might find that they are more cerebral and like to use their cognitive skills to attack a problem.

If a person leads with their feet, they might be telling you that they are a little cautious and aren't going to jump into anything quickly, not exposing themselves until they find that the coast is clear.

These are all examples of the ways that body language can be analyzed. Remember, body language is an art. In purveying it and reading it, you must remember to use artfulness and artful considerations when encountering this.

There are no formulas, there is only intuition. You must develop the side of you that can intuitively read people and trust that part of you through the process. There are some archetypes that you can look for in deciphering body language. These are archetypes that people play into in their personalities. Sometimes, they are accurate, while sometimes, there is more to the story.

First, there is the "cop" archetype. The "cop" archetype may be found in parents, authoritarian figures, and other people who intimidate us. The cop's posture is big and tall, with the chest puffed out and the head relatively straight. A cop's abdomen must always be strengthened, almost flexed, and the arms must be ready to grab for tools around the waist.

This is a certain posture that shows the attitude of alertness, aggression, and strength. This archetype can be called upon to remember the body language characteristics of a person who fits these archetypes. The facial expression will be stern and serious. The head may reach in but is always cautious.

The next archetype for body language is the nerd. The "nerd" is submissive in nature, except in places where they feel very comfortable, and the nerd is always trying to protect him or herself. The nerd has broken down shoulders that do not convey strength. Eye contact is scarce with this type.

The nerd will always find ways to not engage, to be avoidant, to look away, or to move their body to other places to avoid contact with most people in the world. The nerd is not experienced with interaction. However, when the nerd is in his or her element, they will size up and appear bigger and stronger. They may inhibit a different personality type when they are with people they trust or when they are partaking in an activity that they enjoy. This is part of reading body language, and it knows when a person is in their element or not in their element.

Another archetype to consider is the "seductress". The seductress has the attitude that she has what everyone wants. She or he might be coy in their words but very suggestive in their body language. They might decide to wear clothes that accentuate their physical figure, and they might like to tease and play with the body, showing certain parts to certain people.

The seductress will know exactly when to reveal themselves to the people around them and when to keep quiet. They are very good at getting what they want, and they leverage their power as an attractive person into getting what they want. The body language characteristics involved in this person will involve a lot of touching and a lot of physical proximity.

The seductress will know how to impart a physical sense of closeness to the people that they want to be with, and they will simulate a relationship with almost everyone that they want to. They are usually good at manipulating people, especially those who are lonely or afraid.

They will often lead with the hips or breasts, and they will be very visible in a room. These are the type of people who like to make an entrance. You will know when they enter a room.

Another body language archetype is the "old lady". This is the traditional archetype of an old lady, who has completed her life tasks and is very satisfied with her. This is a person who understands her grace and elegance and has a lot of experiences.

However, she is not concerned with getting what she wants, as she has mostly already gotten what she wants out of life. Rather, the "old lady" is satisfied and looks more to social interaction. She will be very strong on eye contact and smiley and will have bright facial expressions that are delighted to encounter another person. She will lead gracefully with the hips, but not forcefully so. Something to look out in the body language of this archetype is their facial expression, as older people will often experience a flattening to their effect.

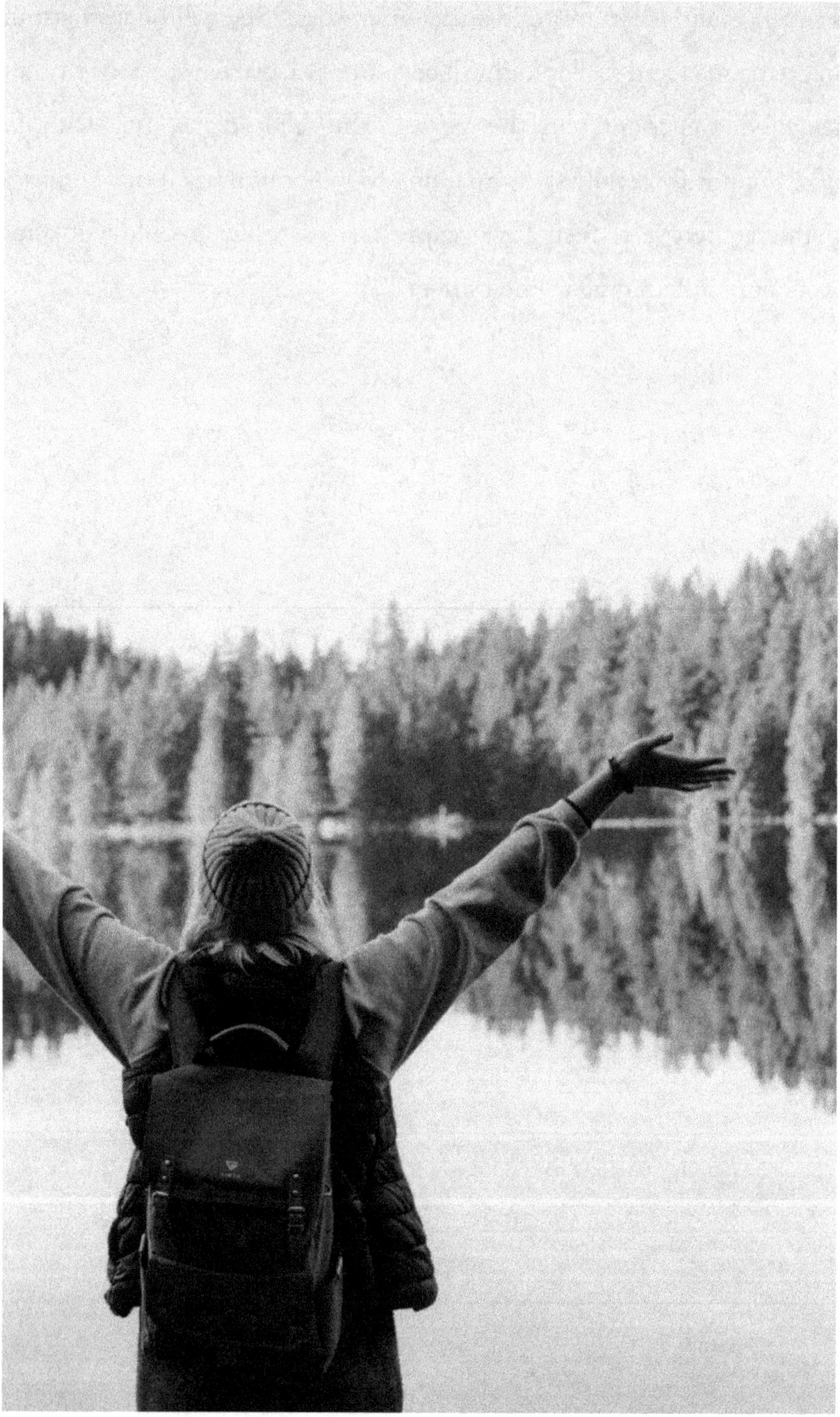

Chapter 7:

Main guidelines for reading and analyzing people

We should all have a certain level of social cognition that will enable us to better understand and help the people around us. Since we are group animals who need others to survive, it's important that we know how to fit into this world. That's not an easy thing to do, but it can still be helpful to our survival to meet other people like us and make deeper connections with those that we can relate to.

When you use tactics to try and get a better understanding of how people operate, it makes it easier to predict what they might do or how they might act. Rather than trying to guess your way through this life, always wondering how other people are feeling, you can really start to take charge and better understand even the most complex people that you meet. This will help you throughout your life, but it will also enable you to help others. We all have loved ones who might be struggling who we wish we could help more, but that can sometimes be difficult. If you start to analyze people and better grasp where it is that they're coming from, you're giving yourself the chance to look for ways that you can actually help them.

There might actually be evolutionary purposes as to why it is that we, as humans, ensure that we can pick up and learn from the behavior of other people. A leopard doesn't teach its cub how to hunt by sitting it down and talking through the steps. The best way that these animals learn is to start with something small and work their way up, all the time watching their parents do the killing first to give them an idea of how it works. These mirror brain methods of comprehension also help us to pick up valuable information just like the animals that watch others to learn.

As we grow older, you can start to pick up on more of your surroundings. You often learn from the actions of those that teach you while you grow. It's important to understand all the ways that you learn about both yourself and other people when you sit down and really start to understand the many ways that the human brain really operates. You will be more in tune with various signals that help give you a better understanding overall rather than taking information at face value.

Many people will not actually say the things that are on their minds. Sometimes it is hard to express ourselves using only the words that we already know. We aren't always taught to express ourselves in healthy ways, so we might simply not know how to do that.

There are situations where it can just be plain scary to open up and say what's on our minds. This difficulty in communication can lead to some very toxic and damaging relationships, so the better equipped we are to speak to one another, the easier it will be to navigate through life.

When you can learn to pick up on both verbal and non-verbal cues, it becomes easier to understand the intention of what others actually desire. At first, you might still miss some signs of people manipulating you. You might also realize that you are paranoid at times and looking too deep into signals that don't actually mean anything. Communication is a practice that not everyone will be perfect at, so don't feel discouraged if it takes a while to get used to understanding dark psychology.

The more you learn to analyze and understand people, the easier it becomes to manipulate them as well. This is to be done in a positive and influential way, of course. Let's discuss more in-depth about why analyzing people can be important.

Why Use Manipulation?

Manipulation is an easy way to get people to do what you want. If you are someone with power, physical strength, or a lot of money, you are already equipped to be more influential. Here's the issue, however. You could boss people around, tell them what to do, and intimidate others into listening to you. This can be easily done depending on your status in life. However, none of these types of manipulation is going to be substantial enough to last. Eventually, many people will realize the control that is happening and will be less easily persuaded. Others will be afraid and want to escape.

You'll no longer want to manipulate people for negative reasons. If you really want long-lasting influence, it has to be done in a positive way. Others will be more influenced by you and have a greater level of respect when you are able to share a positive influence with them.

If you are a highly aware individual, then you will be able to use your influence for good and help to change things to make the world a better place. An influencer is someone who strives to be more of an equal with the people they are persuading. You will have a time when communication can occur, and you can be open with the other person. This will allow both of you to grow, and even when you don't know if what you're doing is the best choice, you will have an open dialogue with others that will help to keep the group moving in the right direction. A manipulator will think that they know exactly what's best for everyone, and even if they realize they are wrong halfway through, they will still do their best to ensure that they prove their point.

You will actually learn a lot about yourself from what you learn from other people. Sometimes you really need an outsider's perspective to grasp the reality of the situation you are the center of. They might be able to help you be more aware of the situation, or they might have gone through something similar that gives you insight into your own scenario.

You can help to break through the boundaries that people might have not been so willing to change in the past. You can help to show a positive influence and the way that it can transform lives for the better, enabling healthy relationships to form between you and those that you are closest to.

Manipulation will enable you to finally speak up for yourself and say what's on your mind. Rather than being a passive person who is afraid to stick up for themselves, you can be more willing to express your opinions, giving you the strength to stick up for yourself.

You can start to get to know people on a deeper level as you tap into their subconscious beyond just what you've discussed in the past. It can be easy to get defensive and turn away from someone, but when you really dive deep into the "why" behind emotions, it can end up bringing you and the other person closer in the end.

All of these reasons we discussed are why it is important that we learn how to use manipulation but in the positive form of persuasion.

How to Protect Yourself Against Persuasion

We all have times when we've been easily influenced by others. Maybe you accidentally signed up for something you never would have if you'd been given more time to think about it.

Maybe someone even swindled you or tricked you into a deal that ended up leaving you with the short end of the stick. Don't feel bad if this has happened to you. It's time now to become much more aware of the way that we can protect ourselves in certain situations.

Sometimes it is not so bad to let other people make decisions. It's nice every once in a while to have another person just make the decisions about what to watch on TV that night or what to eat for dinner. Not every night, of course, but there are some instances when we just might struggle to make decisions.

However, we should still always be as aware as possible of the ways in which we might be falling under someone else's persuasion. The first thing you can do to resist persuasion is to avoid the person trying to persuade you altogether.

If you notice that they might be someone who is trying to trick you into doing something, then it's important to keep your guard up right away.

Next, you can try to put up a defense. Make them question what they're trying to sell to you. If you really aren't sure whether or not you're being manipulated, always ask more questions. Make sure you know the who/what/why/when/where of everything that you might sign up for.

Be highly aware of both the positives and the negatives. Ask "what's the catch?" whenever something seems too good to be true. Make the manipulator face the truth so that they are exposed, and you are more protected.

Ask for some time to think when you feel pressure in the situation. If they aren't willing to give you a second to think without a substantial reason for needing the urgency, then it's a sign they are trying to trick you.

If someone says, "unfortunately, you don't have time," always ask, "why?" If they give you a valid reason, such as a time period is ending or there's a greater risk on the line, then, of course, act as you should.

However, a lot of deals can wait at least until the next morning, so you really have time to think things through.

Don't be afraid to say "no." It can be so hard to say "no" to certain people. Maybe they don't seem to take "no" for an answer, or perhaps they have been so kind and accommodating that you would feel guilty saying "no." Don't let this happen!

No means no, and if you said it once, you shouldn't have to say it again. Don't let others shame you for saying "no!" One of the best ways to protect yourself is to be confident and assured in your own core values. This can be done by developing your levels of emotional intelligence.

Emotional Intelligence

It is crucial that we all can reach a certain level of emotional intelligence. Your IQ is your ability to think intellectually and logically. Your emotional intelligence (EQ) is based more around your abilities to understand and recognize the feelings and emotions of those around you.

In order to have a high level of emotional intelligence, you need to be aware of what your emotions are and where they started to form. The first way to start to become more emotionally intelligent is to always ask "why." Why is it that you are sad? Angry? Jealous? Scared?

When you have these more challenging emotions, always question where they came from and what purpose they are serving.

Ensure that you are separating the emotion from the reaction. If you are angry, you can either react by being quiet or punching a wall. The emotion is the same, but it is the reaction that is positive or negative.

Being angry or sad, or any other challenging emotion is not a bad thing. It's when you don't think your reaction through that things can get tricky. Someone with a high EQ knows how to react to their emotions in a healthy way, whereas those with a low EQ often act only on impulses.

Always question your emotions and make sure that you are really looking deep within yourself. Did this emotion develop in the past? Is it a thought process you were taught? Is it something newer that you have developed?

Start to listen better to others as well. Really actively engage in what they are saying and don't just sit there and try to plan out what you are going to say next. Listen to their words and the subtext in between.

Voice your opinion and be honest with your feelings. As long as you are not hurting anyone in the process, you should always express how you are feeling. If you bottle up your emotions, then you will only hurt yourself mentally and physically down the line.

Remember to view things objectively. Don't label everything as either "positive" or "negative." There is plenty in between, and you will be able to find both a good and bad side to most things if you look hard enough.

Strive for this ambiguity rather than putting everything in one box or the other. Control your immediate reactions. Let yourself process your feelings for a moment before deciding to react. When you start to improve on this, it becomes that much easier to protect yourself from manipulation.

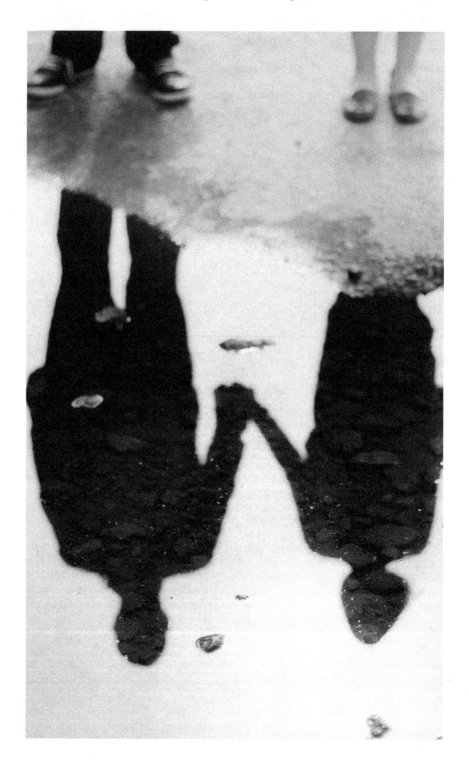

Chapter 8:

Manipulating the mind through NLP

NLP, the mind, and ultimate control

Have you ever wondered how some people are able to handle change constructively and creatively? While some people are knocked off balance by changes in their lives, others seem to fit right in perfectly.

Why is it that some people seem to be in the right place at the right time? How comes some people have good relationships while others cannot get it together even for a week? Is there some form of good luck or inborn traits, making some people more successful than others?

One of the professors at the University of California called John Grinder, and his student called Richard Bandler started to work on a behavioral study project in the 1970s. They observed the behaviors of successful people and were more interested in why some people so good at what they do when compared to others. The findings helped them to develop the neurolinguistics programming, which involved observing, codifying, and replicating the behaviors and thought patterns of successful people. The programming explores the relationship between our neuro (how we think) linguistic (how we communicate) and programs (pour patterns of emotions and behaviors).

The background of Neuro-linguistic programming is that positive behaviors that lead to success can be copied. The professor and the student were interested in the difference between the thought patterns, behaviors, and language use of successful and unsuccessful people.

Their findings are the basis of NLP today. Simply put, the researchers claimed that success has very little to do with luck. You do not have to be lucky in order to succeed. Changing your approaches to life can help you to become more successful in relationships, career, social spec, and other situations. Though some people develop natural ways of becoming successful, these ways of thinking, acting, and speaking can be learned by anyone who is willing to give it a shot.

The Neurolinguistics programming was developed years ago, but a lot of redefinition has taken place over the years. Currently, NLP has become a commonly used technique in self-development and therapy. It is used in education, business, military, and above all, for individuals. NLP can be successfully applied in personal life, and a lot of big companies train their staff on how to use NLP with clients.

Basically, NLP is about how we develop mental representations sounds, images, and verbal descriptions of different situations. When we become aware of the internal maps of reality within us, it becomes easier to consciously change our inner landscape and consequently respond differently to people and situations in the outside world.

One of the main benefits of using NLP is that results can be seen very quickly. For instance, people with some kinds of phobias can be treated in a matter of minutes using some of the techniques found in NLP. Further, blockages and fears can be dealt with easily and quickly through the use of NLP. Honestly speaking, NLP has shed a lot of light on how we interact with our physical and social environments and other aspects of life.

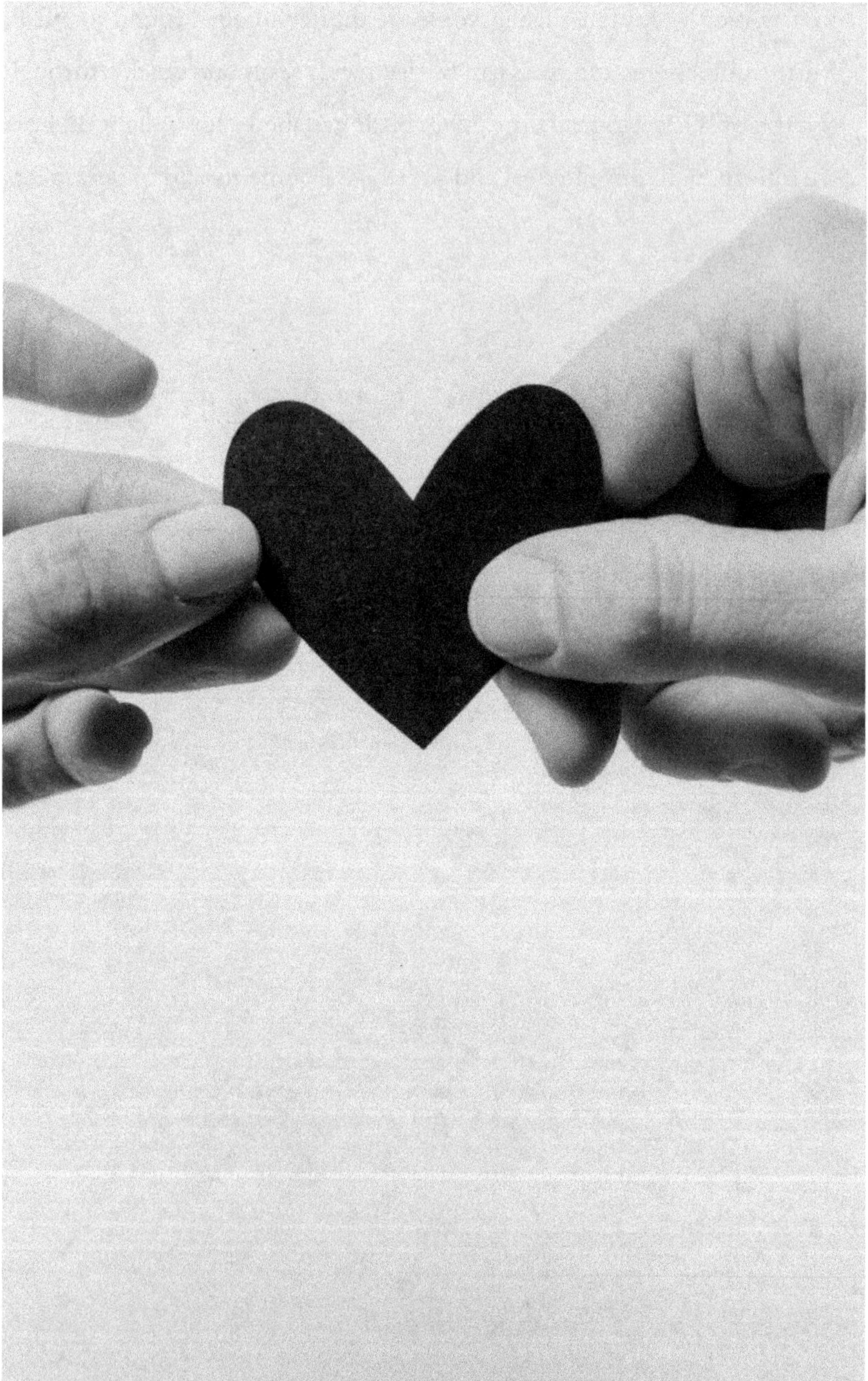

Chapter 9:

Using NLP to avoid manipulation

T he only time when manipulation is considered successful is the time when you allow it to control your emotions and thoughts. Thus, you must start to distinguish what is going on in you that allows you to be easily manipulated by other people. The three most basic reasons we let ourselves to be manipulated are as follows:

- **Fear**

This emotion comes in numerous structures. We, as human beings, tend to fear losing a relationship; we may fear the disapprobation of other people; we dread to make somebody discontent with our actions. We additionally dread the dangers and outcomes of the manipulator's actions. Imagine a scenario in which they really prevail at doing what they threaten.

- **Guilt**

Today, we are clouded by the idea and responsibility that we should dependably prioritize the needs and wants of other people rather than our own. At times when people would talk about the right to fulfill their own needs and wants, manipulators frequently abuse us and endeavor to allow us to feel like we are accomplishing something immoral in the event that we do not generally put their needs and wants in front of our own.

Those individuals who are skilled at these manipulative tactics would tend to define love as the act of fulfilling their needs and wants as part of your obligation. Hence, in the event that we have an opinion that goes against their beliefs, we are manipulated into thinking that we are heartless; at this point, they would make us feel very regretful of our existence and would use guilt to manipulate us.

- **Being too nice**

We appreciate being a provider, fulfilling individuals, and dealing with the needs of other people. We discover fulfillment. Moreover, our confidence would regularly originate from doing what we can for other people.

In any case, at times when there is lack of an unmistakable feeling of these and fair limitations, skilled manipulators are able to detect this in people who are easy targets of this phenomenon and will use certain tactics to further their own selfish gains.

What you need to do to overcome manipulation

We have come to a point where we are here to talk about the basic skills to overcome manipulation. We've stressed the fact that manipulation is only successful if the one being manipulated is unaware of the manipulative acts being performed by the manipulator. Moreover, manipulation would only work if you allow them to control you. Much like hypnosis, any hypnosis is actually self-hypnosis. What we are trying to state here is that knowledge that you are being manipulated defeats its entire purpose. For this section of this book, we will discuss some of the most important techniques to overcome manipulation, which is as follows:

• **Establish a clear sense of self**

There is a need to know your identity, what your needs and wants are, what your emotions are, and what you are fond of and not fond of. You must learn to accept these and not become apologetic, as these are the things that make you. At times, we dread that in the event of speaking up, we are viewed by others as egotistical and called out for being selfish. Nevertheless, knowing your identity or what you really need in life is not at all an act of selfishness. Self-centeredness is demanding that you always get what you want or that other has always put your needs and wants first. Similarly, when another person calls you out for not following their orders or fulfilling their needs and wants, they are the ones being selfish, not you.

• Say "no" despite the other person's disapproval

The ability to say "no" despite somebody's objection is a solid demonstration. Individuals who can do this are present in reality. Because in reality, there is no way that we can accommodate all of their needs and wants. When this happens, they will become baffled, even disappointed. However, keep in mind that what they are feeling is part of human nature. Most of these individuals would then forgive and forget. Sound individuals realize that getting what you want all the time is not possible, even when the desires are genuine. In any case, when we cannot endure another person's mistake or objection, it really ends up hard stating "no." It winds up more diligently for us to state it or have limits. Manipulators exploit this shortcoming and use dissatisfaction and objection in extraordinary structures to get us to do what they need.

• Tolerate the other person's negative affect

We can demonstrate compassion for people's pity, hurt, or even annoyance when accommodating them without having the need to back down and reverse our decision. Keep in mind, a solid relationship is described by common minding, shared genuineness, and shared regard. In the event that you are involved with somebody who uses manipulation and unhealthy control consistently, begin to see little propensities that may not be clear to you at first. As you are more grounded, you are better ready to endure how the other individual's negative impact on you is only bringing you down. Thus, this turns into a positive development that liberates you from their manipulative grasps. This will engender a complexity of sorts with the people in your life. It is possible that the manipulator will start to withdraw and consider your time, your emotions, your wants, and your needs, or they will proceed onward to someone else who is an easy target of manipulation practices.

Basic tricks used by manipulators

As soon as you have realized how knowledge of certain truths about yourself can enlighten you to notice manipulative tactics by other people, you will start to divulge from what you are to what a manipulator can do. With that in mind, if you wish to overcome manipulation, you need to be wary of the basic tactics used by manipulators. Once you have a firm grasp as to what you want and what you do not want, you can go head-to-head with a manipulator and even counter some of their most-used techniques. Nevertheless, always keep in mind that as soon as you realize that you are being manipulated, the manipulator loses. It is simply a matter of whether or not you wish to turn the tables and become the manipulator yourself.

- **Accusing your rival of what he is blaming you for**

This is often referred to as the act of pointing to another person's wrongdoing. When enduring an onslaught and experiencing difficulty regarding safeguarding themselves, manipulators tend to reverse the situation. They blame their rival for committing the exact things that they are being blamed for. *"You state that I don't love you! I think it is you who does not cherish me!"*

- **Appealing to power**

Numerous individuals are in wonderment of those in power or authority, or those who have status. What's more intriguing is that there are various images to which individuals experience extraordinary dedication. Remember, those who are easily manipulated admire those who are in power. Moreover, those who are in power are aware of their ability to control others by never criticizing them. Instead, they use complex misleading tactics to maneuver their thoughts and alter their decision-making process.

Rabble-rousers that effectively control individuals realize that the vast majority are promptly deceived along with these statements. As a result, they collaborate themselves with those in power. This entails the need to look for experts and other educated individuals that will support their perspectives or, at least, not criticize them.

Cigarette organizations once enlisted researchers who were arranged to state that there is not any confirmation that these products can cause lung disease; however, they knew that the proof was already there. Cigarette organizations additionally established The American Tobacco Foundation, a group of specialists trying to find the impacts of smoking on a person's wellbeing. However, in all actuality, the analysts were actually trying to shield the interests of the tobacco business under the pretense of a logical idea that smoking is not dangerous. They misled the public beguiling them into believing that they were speaking logically precautionary measures.

- **Appealing to encounter**

Gifted manipulators and con artists, as well as politicians, would often state that they already have experienced or encountered certain situations in their life, which makes them someone who is in power, which can be associated with the previous point. Nevertheless, this appeal to experience provides them with an image of someone who is capable; this may be used to attack their opponent's lack of experience, even though they themselves have experiences that are limited. You can easily identify this manipulation tactic at times when someone is trying to distort their capabilities about a particular subject.

- **Appealing to fear**

People have fears. The unscrupulous manipulators realize a reality that individuals will, in general, respond crudely when any of these feelings of dread are enacted. Subsequently, they speak to themselves as being able to ensure individuals against these dangers, even when they are not capable of doing so. This is the same for when we talked about giving the target a glimpse of how their most desired outcome is achievable, without really providing it to them. Nonetheless, there are politicians and legislators who frequently utilize this methodology to ensure that individuals line up behind administrative experts and do what the legislature – that is, the thing that the government officials – need.

- **Appealing to sympathy**

Manipulators are able to depict themselves and their circumstance to the public in a means to make them feel frustrated about their current situation.

Consider the understudy who, when gone up against the fact that she has not gotten her work done, whimpers, and says, "You don't see how hard my life is. I have so many things to do. It is extremely difficult for me to complete my schoolwork. I am not fortunate like some of my classmates. Since my folks cannot afford to send me to school, I need to work 30 hours every week to pay my own specific manner. When I get back home from work, my flatmate plays music until late at night, so it is difficult for me to get a good night's sleep. What am I expected to do? Offer me a reprieve!"

Utilization of this ploy empowers the manipulator to occupy consideration from those individuals who may be going through the same thing. Nevertheless, appealing to sympathy is a tactic that most politicians would use to redirect the attention of the public to matters that do not affect their demise.

- ## Appealing to well-known interests

Manipulators and tricksters are always mindful as to how they introduce themselves as persons who possess the right qualities and perspectives among the group of spectators, particularly, the sacred beliefs of the crowd. Everybody has a few partialities, and a great many people feel contempt toward a person or thing. Experts manipulators tend to stir up contempt and prejudices among the crowd.

They suggest that they concur with the group of spectators. They go about as though they have shared ideologies. They attempt to persuade the group of spectators that their enemy does not regard sacred the ideologies that they hold sacred. There is numerous potential in this technique. A particular technique named as the "Just Plain Folks Fallacy" is when an individual infers something along the lines of:

"It is comforting to be back in my home, and with people I can truly trust. It's incredible to be with those who face things squarely; those who utilize their presence of mind to achieve things; individuals who don't have confidence in highfalutin methods for thinking and acting."

- ## Appealing to confidence

This technique is firmly identified with the past points; yet, it stresses what appears to have breezed through the trial of time. Individuals are regularly oppressed by the social traditions and standards of their way of life, just as social conventions. What is conventional to most tend to appear as if it is the correct decision? It is important to note that manipulators infer how they regard sacred the ideologies and beliefs that the group of spectators is familiar with. These individuals suggest that their enemy aims to obliterate the customs, as well as social conventions. Moreover, they do not stress over whether or not these conventions hurt guiltless individuals.

They make the presence of being autonomous in the crowd's perspectives; yet, it would typically be the exact opposite thing. There is a realization that individuals are generally suspicious of the individuals who conflict with present social standards and built up conventions. They realize enough to stay away from these. As a result, there is a kind of restriction on how social traditions are unwittingly and carelessly bound.

• **Begging the inquiry**

One simple approach to demonstrate a point is to accept it in any case. Think about this model:

"Well, what type of government do you want, a government by liberal do-gooders that is able to shell out your hard-earned dollars or a government controlled by business minds that knows how to live within a strict budget and generate jobs that put people to work?"

The previously mentioned statement incorporates the accompanying suppositions that ought not to be underestimated that (1) a liberal government would burn through cash incautiously and that (2) agents realize how to live inside a limited spending plan and produce occupations that set individuals to work.

One minor departure from this error has been classified as "question-begging epithets," the utilization of expressions is actually a prejudgment of an issue by the manner in which it is allowed. In an instance, "Shall we defend freedom and democracy or cave into terrorism and tyranny?" Through the inquiry along these lines, we abstain from discussing awkward inquiries like: "Yet, would we say we are truly propelling human opportunity? Are we truly democratic or simply expanding our capacity, our control, our predominance, our access to foreign markets?" Keep in mind that the statements individuals utilize when bringing about the truth concerning an issue. There is the regular choosing of statements that surmise the accuracy of the situation on the particular issue.

• **Creating a false dilemma**

A genuine problem happens when we are compelled to pick between two similarly unsuitable choices. A false dilemma happens when we are convinced that we have just two, similarly inadmissible decisions, when we truly have multiple potential outcomes accessible to us. Think about the accompanying case: ***"Either we will lose the war on terrorism, or we should surrender a portion of our traditional freedoms and rights."***

Individuals are frequently prepared to acknowledge a false dilemma since few are agreeable with the complex qualifications. Clearing absolutes is actually a part of their manipulative tactics. There is a need to have clear and basic decisions.

• **Hedging what you state**

Manipulators frequently hole up behind words, declining to submit themselves or give straightforward replies or answers. This enables them to withdraw at times of need. Whenever they are found forgetting data significant to the current situation, they would think of some other reason for not being able to come up with said information. At the end of the day, when forced, they may be able to give in; however, to be an excellent manipulator, you should renege on your missteps, conceal your mistakes, and gate keep what you state at whatever point conceivable.

• **Oversimplifying the issue**

Since most people are uncomfortable at comprehending profound or unobtrusive contentions, there are those who are fond of oversimplifying the issue to further their potential benefit. *"I couldn't care less what the measurements inform us concerning the purported abuse of detainees; the main problem is whether we will be tough on crime. Spare your compassion toward the criminals' victims, not for the actual criminals."* The reality being overlooked is that the maltreatment of criminals is a crime in itself. Tragically, individuals with an over-simple mindset could not care less about criminal conduct that victimizes criminals.

- **Raising only complaints**

Your adversary is giving valid justifications to acknowledge a contention; however, the truth of the matter is that your mind is made up and nothing can change it. Gifted manipulators would react with objections after objections. As their rivals answer one protest after another, they would proceed again to object and object. The implicit mentality of the manipulator is that *"regardless of what my rival says, I will continue to object because nothing else will convince me otherwise."*

- **Rewriting history**

The most noticeably awful acts and outrages tend to vanish from chronicled accounts while false dreams can be made to become facts. This phenomenon is often observed with Patriotic History. The composition of a contorted type of history is supported by the adoration of the nation and regularly defended by the charge of the antagonism. The truth of the matter is that our mind is persistently attempting to re-portray occasions of the past to absolve itself and denounce its spoilers. Chronicled composing frequently goes with the same pattern, particularly in the composition of reading material for schools. In this way, in recounting to an anecdote about what has happened, those who perform manipulative tactics do not hesitate to contort the past in the manners in which they accept they can pull off. As usual, the manipulator is prepared with self-justifying excuses.

- **Shifting the burden of proof**

This act alludes to when an individual has the obligation to demonstrate some of his declarations. A good example would be the instance that happened inside a court. The examiner possesses the obligation to prove guilt past distrust. Furthermore, the defense should not claim the responsibility of having to prove innocence. Those who are capable of manipulating others do not have the need to assume the weight of evidence for what they attest to. Along these lines, they harness the right tool in shifting the burden of proof to their rivals.

- **Talking in vague generalities and statements**

It is difficult to refute individuals when they cannot be bound. So, as opposed to concentrating on specifics, those who are capable of manipulating others tend to speak in the most unclear phrases that they can pull off. We have already talked about how certain statements and generalities can put another person in a daze, which makes it easier for them to be manipulated. This misrepresentation is well known with politicians. For instance, *"Overlook what the cowardly liberals say. It's the right time to be tough, to be hard on criminals, to punish terrorists, and be tough on those who disparage our nation."* Manipulators ensure they do not utilize particulars that may make individuals question what they are doing in the first place.

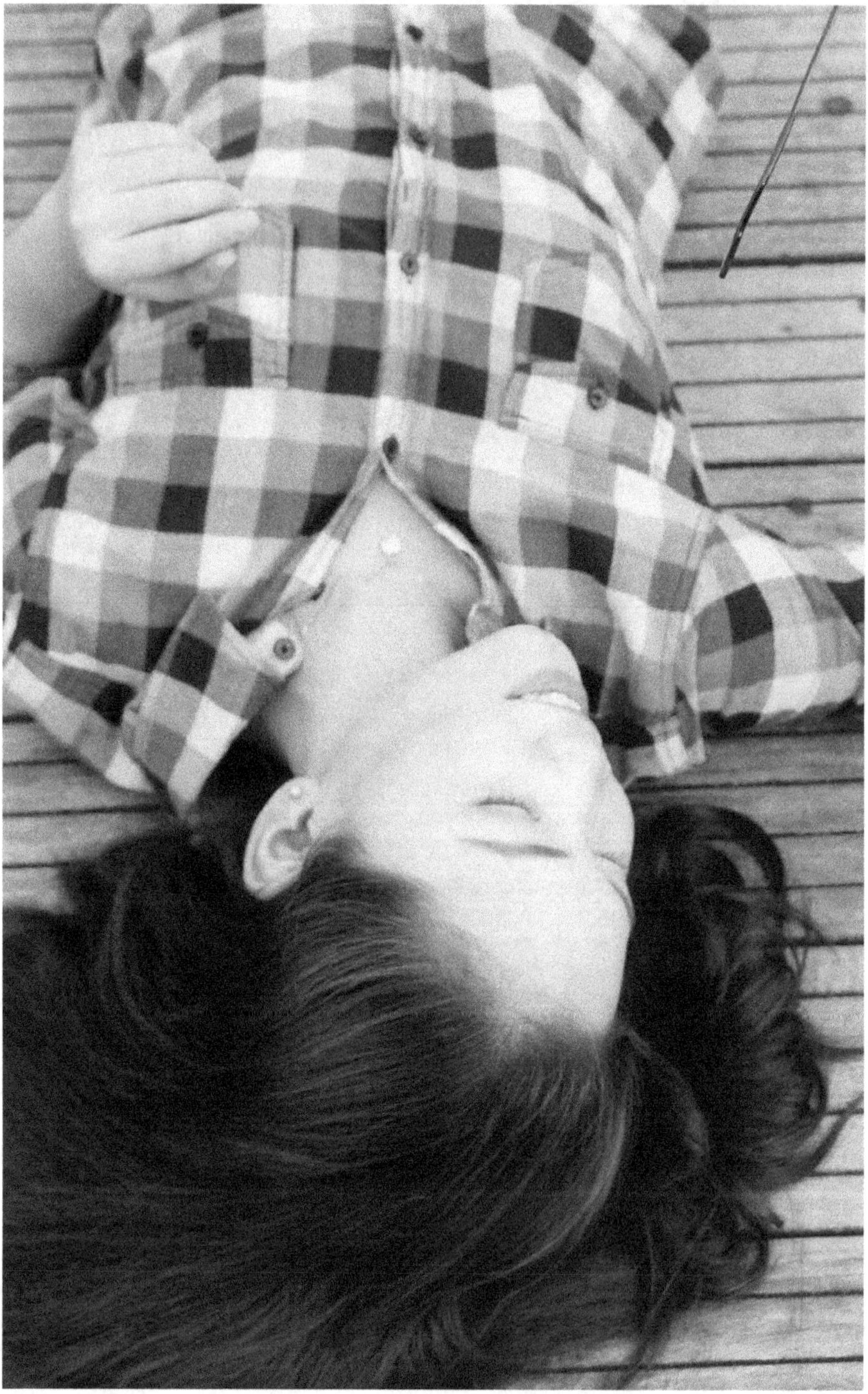

Conclusion

Neuro-linguistic programming is truly a brilliant discovery. It can be used to accomplish anything you desire. NLP goes beyond self-help. It actually allows you to transform yourself and become a better person.

You no longer need to procrastinate goals and hate yourself. If you start using NLP today, you can become the person you always wanted to become. The ability to accomplish all of your dreams already lies inside of you. Now you just have to overcome your mental blocks and hurdles to unleash your inner abilities.

The world of NLP is quite vast. There are NLP techniques for overcoming any fear or mental block and for improving any skill. You can use NLP to get over breakups, smoking, and a bad temper. Anything you want to achieve is possible with NLP.

With such limitless possibility, you can have the life, the body, and the personality that you want. You just need to learn how. This book is your introduction to the power of NLP. It will allow you to master yourself and achieve inner peace. It will show you how to achieve goals and become the best possible version of yourself to others. You can use this book to both tackle your goals and make more lucrative acquaintances.

Manipulation Mastery

CPSIA information can be obtained
at www.ICGtesting.com
Printed in the USA
BVHW040318120521
607043BV00001B/144